4/99

D1207308

The Roman Colosseum

MIKAYA PRESS

NEW YORK

*To The Writers Room, with gratitude for the invaluable
hours of companionable solitude.*

*Thanks to Norma Goldman, College of Lifelong Learning, Wayne State University,
Detroit, Michigan for her patient and painstaking review of the manuscript.
(Remaining errors of fact and interpretation are the author's alone.)*

OTHER BOOKS BY ELIZABETH MANN

The Brooklyn Bridge
The Great Pyramid
The Great Wall
The Panama Canal

Editor: Stuart Waldman
Design: Lesley Ehlers Design

Copyright ©1998 Mikaya Press
Original Illustrations Copyright © Michael Racz
All rights reserved. Published by Mikaya Press Inc.
Wonders of the World Books is a registered trademark of Mikaya Press Inc.
No part of this publication may be reproduced in whole or in part or stored in a retrieval system, or transmitted
in any form or by any means, electronic, mechanical, photocopying,recording or otherwise, without written
permission of the publisher. For information regarding permission, write to:
Mikaya Press Inc.,12 Bedford Street, New York, N.Y.10014.
Distributed in North America by: Firefly Books Ltd., 3680 Victoria Park Ave., Willowdale, Ontario, M2H3KI

Library of Congress Cataloging -in-publication Data
Mann, Elizabeth, 1948-
The Roman Colosseum / by Elizabeth Mann ; with illustrations by Michael Racz.
p.   cm.– (A wonders of the world book)
Includes index.
Summary: Describes the building of the Colosseum in ancient Rome, and tells how it was used.
ISBN 0-9650493-3-7 (hardcover)
1. Colosseum (Rome, Italy)—Juvenile literature.
2. Amphitheaters—Rome—Juvenile literature. 3. Rome (Italy)–
–Buildings, structures, etc.—Juvenile literature. 4. Rome (Italy)–
Antiquities—Juvenile literature.[1. Colosseum (Rome, Italy)
2. Rome (Italy)— Antiquities.] 1. Title. ll. Series.
DG68. 1. M27 1998
937' .6—dc21   98-20060
                                                          CIP
                                                          AC

Printed in Singapore

The Roman Colosseum

A WONDERS OF THE WORLD BOOK

BY ELIZABETH MANN
WITH ILLUSTRATIONS BY MICHAEL RACZ

MIKAYA PRESS

NEW YORK

Emperor Titus Flavius was stunned by the noise that filled the amphitheater as he rose to his feet and stepped to the front of his box. The animals, musicians, dancers, charioteers, and gladiators parading around the arena had received thunderous applause from the audience, but now the roar was even louder. Fifty thousand spectators howled with pleasure at the sight of the emperor, their host at this most lavish entertainment. Deafened, but very pleased, Titus slowly raised his hands in a salute to his subjects. Trumpets blared and the cheering echoed. The Flavian Amphitheater, the Colosseum, was officially open. The celebration, 100 days of festivities and entertainment, could begin.

Romans had their own ideas of what entertainment should be. Gymnastics and foot races, the kinds of athletic competitions favored in neighboring Greece, had never caught on in Rome. Stage plays, whether tragedy or comedy, seemed a tame reflection of life. To please a Roman audience, real blood had to be shed. Real people and animals had to die. Titus knew that, and he had planned spectacles for the opening of the amphitheater to satisfy the most demanding crowd.

The morning's entertainment began. Lions fought against elephants and enraged bulls. Trees, boulders, and other scenery appeared, transforming the arena into a woodland setting. Leopards were released and hunters pursued and killed them. Crocodiles, ostriches, boars, and elephants were slaughtered. Hours later the wild beast shows ended. The crowd talked excitedly during the pause for a midday meal. The best was still to come.

Again trumpets sounded, and a procession of gladiators entered the arena. They were well-trained and well-armed, the best that Rome's gladiatorial schools had to offer. As they stopped before the emperor's box, the crowd grew silent. The gladiators solemnly greeted Titus: "We who are about to die salute you."

Pair after pair of gladiators clashed in skilled hand-to-hand combat. They were fighting for their lives, and they fought furiously. The audience cheered them on. As corpses were dragged out through the *Porta Libitina* (Gate of the Dead) at the eastern end of the arena, more gladiators strutted in at the western end. Slaves raked fresh sand over the blood-soaked arena floor (arena comes from the Latin word for sand—*harena*) and the combat continued.

When the last fight had ended, the few victorious gladiators were rewarded. Titus presented each with a palm branch—symbol of victory—and gold coins. The spectators, weary but satisfied, trailed out into the night. The first day was over. Ninety-nine more days lay ahead.

An attendant dressed as the ancient Etruscan god of the dead, Charun, used a mallet to to symbolically claim fallen fighters for the land of the dead. Then other costumed attendants dragged the bodies from the arena to a room called the spoliarium. *There, their costly helmets and armor were stripped off and saved to be used again.*

Romans had not always been the bored, restless thrill-seekers that the Emperor Titus entertained. By nature they were an ambitious and enterprising people. For centuries, they had poured their great energy into the conquest of new territory. Roman farmers readily left their fields to become soldiers, and they were very successful. They established settlements in distant lands, and built roads linking the settlements with Rome. Rome grew from a small town on the banks of the Tiber River into the capital city of a vast empire. Roman territory at its largest extended from the cold, misty forests of northern England to the burning sands of Egypt, from Spain in the west along both coasts of the Mediterranean to the Middle East. Eventually one fifth of the world's people would come under Roman control.

Romans were a warlike people, and had been from their very beginnings. The mythological twins, Romulus and Remus, who were said to have founded Rome in 725 B.C., were descended from Mars, the god of war. In 509 B.C., the Roman Republic was established as a result of a war against the Etruscans, people who lived to the north of the city of Rome. For centuries after that, whether they were defending themselves against encroaching enemies or acquiring new lands, Romans had known little peace. Warfare was a way of life and an important aspect of their religion. They respected courage and fighting skills and valued the rigorous military training and harsh discipline that created a successful army.

Gladiatorial combat was an exciting display of everything the Romans most admired. They appreciated the discipline and hard work necessary to produce well-trained gladiators, and they applauded their skill and courage. For Romans, the thrill of the arena was the next best thing to going to war.

As this magnificent relief carving shows, Romans celebrated death and slaughter, as well as military victory, in their artwork.

Gladiatorial fights hadn't always been public entertainment. They had begun as a somber Etruscan religious ritual. The Etruscans believed that a dead person's soul was comforted if blood was shed in its honor. In wartime, blood was provided for the souls of comrades killed in battle by forcing captured enemy soldiers to fight to the death. Like many Etruscan customs, this one was adopted by the Romans.

The custom was probably introduced into Rome for the first time in 264 B.C. Two brothers had three pairs of slaves fight to the death at their father's funeral. The idea caught on, and so began the Roman tradition of *munera,* battles given as gifts at funerals to honor the dead.

Often traditions that begin as serious religious rites change as time passes, and so it was with the *munera.* Aristocratic families began to hold *munera* to celebrate occasions other than funerals. They invited the public to attend, and offered them food and gifts as well as entertainment. Hosting a *munera* was expensive, but by welcoming the common people, a wealthy aristocrat was being clever, as well as generous. He was rewarded many times over by the popular approval and good will that he and his family enjoyed after a successful *munera.*

Munera *took place in cattle markets, town squares, or any public space that could hold a crowd.*

During the period called the Republic, Rome had a representative form of government. Citizens had the right to vote for the people who governed them, but the Roman Republic could never be mistaken for a modern democracy. Women, for example, were not represented. Slaves, a group whose numbers grew dramatically as newly captured prisoners of war were added, had no rights at all.

The most powerful part of the government was the Senate. Only *patricians* (wealthy aristocrats) could become senators. *Plebeians* (common people) elected *tribunes* to represent them. Some of these politicians sponsored *munera* to influence citizens and win their votes. As a result, gladiatorial shows became bigger and more lavish.

In 65 B.C. an ambitious senator named Julius Caesar changed forever the way public entertainment was presented in Rome. He announced *munera* that promised to be more magnificent than anything seen before. Lions were brought from Africa to appear in the *venationes* (wild animal shows). More pairs of gladiators were scheduled to fight than ever before. The armor would be splendid, the weapons coated with silver. For weeks, Romans could talk of nothing else.

The spectacle was designed to overwhelm the people of Rome, and it was wildly successful. Caesar's popularity soared, and his influence increased tremendously. It was a step in his long climb to power, and he went on to win higher and higher political offices. Caesar was a general as well as a politician, and the victories won by his fiercely loyal armies increased his prestige and power. He celebrated his triumphs lavishly, using the spoils of war to stage bigger and better *munera.* Between his grand spectacles and his military success, he became the most powerful man in government.

By 44 B.C., the Senate was so intimidated by Caesar that they gave him the unheard of position of dictator for life. Never before during the Republic had one man had such great power. A group of senators, regretful of the authority that they had granted Caesar and eager to restore the Republic, began to plot against him. A month later they surrounded Caesar and stabbed him to death.

Caesar built up the excitement before his munera *with displays like this in the Forum, a public area in the center of Rome .*

But Caesar's death did not restore the Republic. In fact, his short reign as dictator had the opposite effect. It marked the end of nearly four centuries of a representative form of government. It paved the way for future leaders to become all-powerful emperors.

By the time Julius Caesar's heir, Augustus, took over in 27 B.C., the Roman Republic no longer existed. In its place was the Roman Empire, and Augustus was its first emperor. His power was absolute. The citizens of Rome no longer had a say in the government.

Augustus knew that sponsors of gladiatorial games could become popular and influential and possibly a threat to his position. He wanted to make sure that he never faced that kind of challenge. He changed the laws so that gladiatorial combat and *venationes* could only take place as part of the annual government festivals honoring Roman gods, and only with his permission. Private citizens, no matter how wealthy, could no longer sponsor games. Traditional funeral *munera* became a thing of the past. The *munera* were transformed into *ludi,* official "games" sponsored and controlled by the emperor. To increase his own popularity and influence over the people, Augustus held more *ludi* than ever. By the end of his reign in 14 A.D., he was sponsoring more than 90 days of *ludi* a year in Rome.

When a wounded gladiator threw down his shield and raised a finger of his left hand asking for mercy, it was up to the sponsor of the games to decide his fate. It was traditional for sponsors to listen to the opinion of the crowd. If the audience turned thumbs up, the sponsor let the gladiator live. If the crowd turned thumbs down, he gave the signal for his throat to be cut. Augustus followed this tradition. He listened to his subjects in the arena, giving them the illusion that they could influence him, but he ignored them in important government decisions.

Augustus devoted himself to the job of ruling the Roman Empire. He used his great power to create a time of peace and prosperity. Emperors who followed him did not rule as wisely. Some, like Nero, are known to this day for their terrible abuse of authority. Nero, who became emperor in 54 A.D., was notoriously intolerant of those who displeased him. He ordered the murders of many people, including his mother and one of his wives, for the smallest offenses.

In 64 A.D., a fire raged through the city, burning much of central Rome to the ground. Instead of rebuilding the homes that the fire destroyed, Nero seized the land for himself. On it he built his enormous *Domus Aurea* (Golden House), a luxurious palace and private garden. This only increased the resentment that his cruelty, irresponsible governing, and wasteful spending had already earned him. Even the Roman army, usually loyal to the emperor, turned against him. Nero was finally forced to give up the throne, and he eventually committed suicide in 68 A.D.

His death triggered a period of conflict and civil war in Rome. Military generals, backed by their legions of loyal soldiers, competed with each other to become emperor. In one year, three different generals won and then quickly lost the title. The city was in an uproar.

Sailors watched the flames from the safety of boats in the Tiber River.

A fourth general, Vespasian Flavius (father of Emperor Titus Flavius), emerged victorious from the civil wars. His soldiers defeated all the opposing armies and made him emperor. It was a great honor, but governing the sprawling empire was a difficult task.

Nero's neglect had allowed the provinces of the Empire to slip from Rome's control. The capital city itself, crammed with a million overcrowded, unruly people, had never recovered from the effects of the terrible fire of 64. Nero's extravagant spending and the chaos that followed his reign had caused widespread poverty in Rome. Many people were unemployed, hungry, and angry. It was a desperate situation.

When Vespasian became emperor he was already a tough and experienced leader. Nearly 70 years old, he had survived decades on the battlefield, as well as the whims of treacherous emperors like Nero. Above all, he was a very practical man, and he tackled the problems of the city in his usual very practical way. He could see that, in order to rule the empire, he had to first bring Rome's people under control. To ease their hunger, he distributed bread. To take their minds off their wretched living conditions, he sponsored frequent *ludi.*

People who were fed and amused were less angry and easier to control. Vespasian wasn't the first or the last emperor to rule by pacifying and distracting his subjects, but he did it very effectively. (A famous Roman writer named Juvenal called this uniquely Roman way of governing "giving the people bread and circuses." The phrase is still used today.)

Vespasian also had to revive the people's confidence in the government. In our time, politicians use newspapers and television to influence public opinion. Vespasian chose to impress the people of Rome through the buildings he erected. Grand and imposing buildings would serve as constant reminders of his greatness.

He decided that his most magnificent building would be an amphitheater. By building the Colosseum, an enormous amphitheater devoted entirely to the *ludi,* he sent a clear message to the people. He not only demonstrated that he had the power to accomplish such a difficult feat, he showed his subjects that he understood what they liked and would provide the entertainment they craved.

The location for Vespasian's amphitheater, on the bed of an artificial lake in the garden of Nero's hated Domus Aurea, *was carefully selected. By building there, Vespasian gave back to the people the land that Nero had taken after the fire. This sent a strong message to the people that now they had an emperor who would take care of them.*

The Colosseum wasn't the first amphitheater in Rome. Temporary wooden ones had been set up in the Forum and dismantled when the games were over. Nor was it the first amphitheater to be made of stone. A smaller one had been built in the city of Pompei in 89 B.C. But the Colosseum was the largest in the world, and, because it was in the capital of the Empire, it was the most important. It was also a masterpiece of architectural design and engineering skill.

One of the greatest obstacles to building this huge and complicated structure was its great weight. If such a massive building was to stand for centuries, as Vespasian hoped, it had to rest on a very solid foundation.

A drainage system was installed to empty the water from Nero's lake into the Tiber River. Then a wide oval trench, 18 feet deep, was dug underneath the area where the seats would eventually be. The trench was filled with solid concrete. The heavy stone and concrete walls would rest on this massive foundation.

Vespasian was in a hurry. He was an old man, and he wanted his amphitheater completed before he died. The architect, unknown to us today, was under tremendous pressure to finish the job quickly, and he devised wonderfully efficient ways of working. The way in which he organized the labor force and construction materials at the Colosseum would look familiar to a 20th century builder.

The amphitheater was divided into quarters. Independent crews of skilled artisans worked simultaneously on each quarter, making the job go faster. A skeleton of supporting walls was built all the way up to the top of the second level and covered with a roof. Once the skeleton was in place, the marble seats, staircases, and arched corridors could be filled in on two levels at the same time.

As big as the amphitheater was, it couldn't contain the hundreds of bustling workers who built the walls and the many stonemasons who shaped the marble seats and stairs. These were made in workshops and then brought to the amphitheater. The pieces were made to be interchangeable—all the stairs were the same width, for example—so they were simpler to install. This use of standardized parts is another thoroughly modern technique that is common in construction today.

This machine was used to lift heavy stone blocks into position. It was powered by slaves walking inside the large wheel and turning it, just as pet mice turn an exercise wheel in a cage.

limestone

concrete

vaulted arches

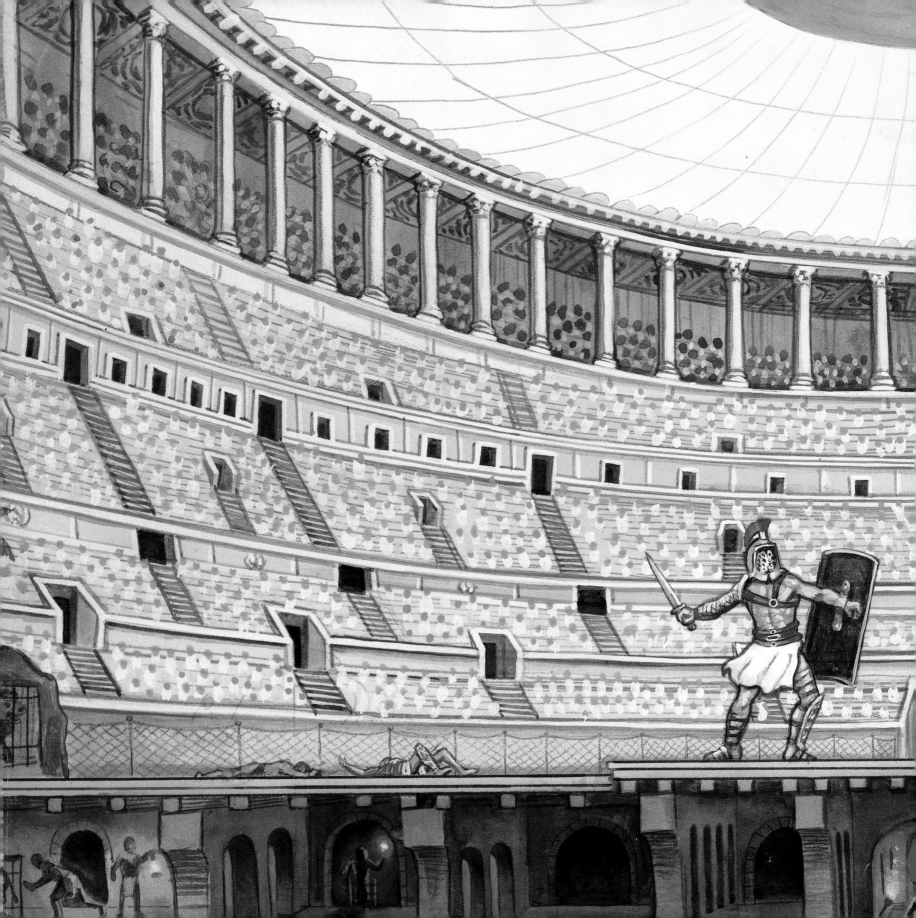

The concrete used in the Colosseum would also look right at home on a modern construction site. Concrete was invented by the Romans in the 2nd century B.C., and it's made the same way now— by mixing lime, sand, and water with stone rubble and allowing it to harden. As it hardens, it doesn't simply dry out. A chemical reaction takes place, and the sand and limestone are bonded tightly together. The result is a rock-like material that is strong, cheap, and easy to use.

Since concrete was a relatively recent invention, the Romans were still learning how to use it when the Colosseum was being built. They weren't sure just how strong this remarkable new material was, and they didn't want to take risks in such an important building. They cautiously combined concrete and stone, an ancient and more trusted material. The ceilings of the corridors that circled the arena on each level were vaulted arches made of concrete, for example, but the supports they rested on were made of strong, heavy limestone.

Vaulted arches themselves were also a Roman invention. The arched shape made them much stronger than a flat ceiling would have been. Vaulted arches made of concrete added strength to the building without adding excessive weight. Without concrete and vaulted arches, the Colosseum couldn't have been built.

Another great challenge for the architect was accommodating the audience. Fifty thousand people had to be comfortable during games that often lasted from morning til night. They had to be able to enter quickly, without pushing and shoving, find their seats easily, and exit just as calmly. Romans were an excitable audience, and the violence they watched in the arena did nothing to soothe them. Any confusion, any arguments or shoving, could easily provoke trouble and fighting in the audience. The crowds had to be controlled. The building itself had to work to control them.

The architect devised an ingenious system of entrances, corridors, and staircases that allowed the crowds to come and go smoothly.

There were 80 separate entrance arches. Two were for gladiators (one for the living, one for the dead), two were for the emperor and other dignitaries. The remaining 76 arches had Roman numerals I through LXXVI carved into the stone above them. These numbers also appeared on admission tickets to help people find their seats. (The *ludi* were a gift from the emperor to the people. Tickets were required, but they were free of charge.)

There were four levels of seating, and each level was divided into sections. Each section on each level had its own staircase that led directly to it. By using so many separate entrances and staircases, the architect neatly solved the problem of crowd control. It's said that all 50,000 people could leave the Colosseum in just three minutes!

Ironically, the name "Colosseum" did not come from Vespasian, but from Nero. Whe Nero built his Domus Aurea he put up a gigantic bronze statue of himself called a Colossus. Although Vespasian wanted to erase all traces of the hated emperor when took the throne, he was too practical to destroy such a fine sculpture. Instead he changed the face to that of the god Apollo. Eventually the Flavian Amphitheater ca to be called the Colosseum, after Nero's giant statue which stood nearby.

People were seated according to their position in society. Upper class people (senators, nobles, and priestesses) sat in the first tier, closest to the arena. Lower classes (slaves and foreigners) sat in higher tiers, far from the action. Most women sat at the very top beneath a wooden roof. Sections in the middle tiers were assigned to people according to their trade, so that weavers sat with weavers and sandal makers sat with sandal makers. The emperor, with his own very visible and luxurious box, was clearly superior to everyone else. In the Colosseum, everyone knew their place and who their superiors were, which is exactly the kind of orderly society Vespasian wanted to see throughout Rome and the Empire.

Despite the speed and efficiency of Vespasian's workers, his amphitheater was unfinished when he died in 79 A.D. Work was still being done on it when his son, Titus Flavius, staged the 100-day opening celebration in 80 A.D. When Titus died, it was up to his younger brother, Domitian Flavius, to finally complete the Colosseum. He built the entire fourth level of seating and added many finishing touches.

Beneath the arena, Domitian built a system of small cells and narrow corridors. Just as the audience was guided through entrances and stairways to their seats, the underground system guided the wild animals through trap doors and on to the arena floor.

Another system of ramps and ropes allowed scenery to appear as if by magic, transforming the arena into a jungle or a battlefield or anything the show called for. Tunnels connected the Colosseum basement to the menageries where the animals were kept and to workshops where the scenery was built.

No matter how fascinating the spectacle, sitting all day long in the blazing sun of southern Italy could have been a miserable experience for the audience. To make his guests comfortable, Domitian installed a *velarium,* an enormous cloth awning. It was suspended from 240 tall wooden masts that stuck up above the outside wall of the Colosseum. A system of ropes and pulleys allowed sections of the *velarium* to be extended over the audience whenever they were needed. Hundreds of sailors were brought to Rome to handle the complicated ropes.

The finished Colosseum was a far cry from the rough wooden amphitheaters that had been built in the Forum in earlier times. Statues filled every niche on the outside of the building. Inside, there were more statues, and fountains, and wall paintings, and soft bright cushions for the marble seats. Polished marble and gold gleamed everywhere. Romans had always enjoyed gladiatorial games. Now they could enjoy them in comfort and luxury.

Keeping the arena supplied with performers was as monumental a task as building the Colosseum.

Hunters combed the farthest reaches of the Empire, and beyond, searching for exotic animals to appear in the *venationes*. Boars and lynxes were captured in northern Europe and brought to Rome in carts. Ships crossed the Mediterranean carrying hippopotamuses and crocodiles from the Nile River and lions and elephants from the African plains. Some animals were trained to do remarkable tricks, like the ones that circus animals perform today. Most were slaughtered soon after arriving at the arena. More and more animals were needed. The demand was so great that some animal species disappeared from large areas in North Africa.

Capturing, transporting, training, and feeding thousands upon thousands of animals was a costly business for Rome's emperors, but a necessary one. The people loved the *venationes*. And, like everything else in the Colosseum, the exotic animals conveyed a message from the emperor. What better reminder of the vast extent of the Empire than the sight of giraffes and rhinoceroses from faraway lands in the Roman arena? What better proof of the emperor's god-like power than the sight of lions trained to hold rabbits gently in their mouths and release them unharmed at his command? It was a dull Roman indeed who would miss the point of these repeated demonstrations of the emperor's might.

Gladiators, the human performers, also came from all parts of the Empire. Some were prisoners of war. Though the Empire was, for the most part, at peace following Augustus's reign, rebellions still flared up in the provinces. Captured rebel soldiers were taken to gladiatorial schools for training. They fought in the imperial *ludi* in Rome, as well as in the nearly 80 smaller arenas believed to have existed in cities throughout the Empire.

Slavery was a way of life in Rome, and slaves made up nearly half of the population. Slaves who worked hard and pleased their owners could earn their freedom, but many ended their lives as gladiators. Owners sold slaves into the gladiatorial schools as punishment, or for any reason at all.

Some people volunteered to be gladiators. Those who did automatically became slaves. Poor and unemployed freemen and freedmen (former slaves) became gladiators despite the danger. An early and horrible death was likely, but the guaranteed food and shelter of the gladiatorial school seemed better than a life of desperate poverty in the crowded Roman slums. Ex-soldiers became gladiators because that was the only work they knew how to do. On rare occasions, wealthy aristocrats fought in the arena, to the delight of the *plebeians,* and to the disgust and shame of their fellow *patricians*. Occasionally women fought as gladiators, but it was unusual.

The arena offered the hope, however slim, of a better life. After years of brave and successful combat, gladiators could receive the *rudis,* a wooden sword symbolizing release from the arena. Sometimes they even won release from slavery. Popular gladiators were well rewarded, and, if they lived long enough, retired in comfort and luxury.

Slaves did much of the work in ancient Rome. Most performed menial tasks. The slaves shown in this mosaic, for example, are pressing oil from olives.

There were four schools in Rome where gladiators and *bestiarii* (animal fighters) were trained. Upon entering a *ludus* (gladiatorial school), each gladiator swore an oath agreeing to suffer whips, burning, and death. The training was rigorous and could last for years. Beginners practiced with wooden sticks on stuffed straw dummies to learn the techniques of swordplay and killing before graduating to blunt iron weapons, and finally to sharp swords. The instructors were former gladiators who had survived many battles in the arena. They taught their students to fight for their lives. And, because Roman audiences liked bravery, they also taught them how to die fearlessly.

Talented gladiators were worth a lot of money and, like valuable livestock, they were carefully tended. They were fed a special barley diet to strengthen their bodies. Skilled surgeons bandaged their wounds, and attendants massaged their sore muscles. The special care did not conceal the fact that they were treated like dangerous animals. Gladiators were prisoners in the schools. Weapons were locked away, and armed guards made sure that they didn't wander out into the city. Any wrongdoing was horribly punished.

New recruits were always needed. Often they were provided by *lanistae,* agents who traveled the provinces buying, selling, and trading promising fighters. Some trained their own troupes of gladiators and rented them out for local gladiatorial shows in the smaller cities of the Empire. The *lanistae* sold their best fighters to the four imperial schools in Rome. The better his gladiators, the better the emperor looked to his subjects.

The largest gladiatorial school in Rome, the Ludus Magnus, *was located just a few hundred feet from the amphitheater. The gladiators paraded through the streets from the* ludus *to the amphitheater, to the delight of fans who hadn't been able to get tickets.*

Each gladiator was trained in a specific fighting style. Each had its own armor, weapons, helmets, and techniques. Some of these different styles were taken from people the Romans had conquered during wars to build the Empire. The *essedarii,* for example, fought from chariots, as soldiers in Britain had once done. The small round shield and short curved sword carried by *Thracians* came from a part of Greece called Thrace. Watching gladiators fight in the manner of these ancient enemies was a way for Romans to relive past military glories.

To make the combat interesting, different types of gladiators were matched against each other. *Retiarii,* who fought with a fishing net and a trident, were paired against *secutores* who carried heavy shields and swords and wore beautifully decorated helmets. *Thracians* fought *hoplomachi,* huge men who carried the most massive shields. Each fighting style had loyal followers who rooted passionately for their favorites. Even emperors were fans.

*The gladiators shown here are, from
left to right, a* hoplomachus, *a*
Thracian, *a* secutor, *and a* retiarius.

Criminals sentenced to the arena as punishment did not have the advantages of the gladiators from the Roman schools. They were forced to fight without training, and sometimes without armor or weapons. If they hesitated, attendants dressed like characters from mythology whipped them or prodded them with red hot metal bars. Their chances of survival were small, and their careers usually ended with their first appearance. A sentence of *damnati ad bestiam* meant that the execution was to be carried out by wild animals. These criminals had no chance.

The horrible executions were intended as a punishment to wrongdoers and as a warning to others, but they were also public entertainment. They were as popular as the *venationes,* and the show had to go on. If many *ludi* were scheduled and there was a shortage of victims, prisoners could find themselves sentenced to die in the arena for minor crimes.

Romans had very mixed feelings about gladiators. Gladiators were slaves, and like all slaves in Rome, were thought of as less than human. Their suffering was not pitied and their brutal deaths were not mourned. Instead of receiving traditional burials, their bodies were often thrown into garbage pits or into the Tiber River.

And yet, in one of the great contradictions of all time, Romans adored and admired successful gladiators. They followed the careers of their favorite fighters and cheered them as avidly as any modern sports fan cheers a winning boxer. Walls, lamps, and baby bottles were decorated with their pictures. They were heroes to *plebeians* and *patricians* alike.

Centuries passed, emperors came and went, but the popularity of the *ludi* never changed. Audiences demanded more and better entertainment, but large, exciting shows were becoming difficult to present. Exotic wild animals were harder to find. Maintaining troupes of gladiators was a costly burden.

Meanwhile, the world was changing. No empire lasts forever, and the Roman Empire was no exception. Barbarian tribes–Huns, Vandals, Goths–threatened on all sides. As the barbarians grew stronger, the Empire had to struggle to defend its borders from their attacks. The defense was expensive, and that meant that there was less money available to spend on the *ludi*.

Within the Empire, the Christian religion was spreading, and traditional Roman ways were being questioned. The *ludi* especially were criticized. The cruel slaughter of the gladiatorial games was dramatically at odds with the teachings of Christianity, which valued human life and taught compassion. As more and more people joined the faith, even some emperors converted. Still, the *ludi* were such an important part of Roman life that they continued even during the reigns of Christian emperors, and some Christians attended the games.

Over the years, the rising costs of the *ludi* and the protests against them began to have an effect, and fewer games were sponsored. In 404, a Christian monk named Telemachus jumped into the arena to stop a gladiatorial fight. The audience, angry at the interruption in the entertainment, tore Telemachus to pieces, but his death was not in vain. The Emperor Honorius was so horrified that he banned fights to the death between humans. Over a century later, in 523, the *venationes* were also banned.

After more than 400 years of activity, the Colosseum was silent. The statues and gold disappeared, and the wooden arena floor rotted away. A wild tangle of plants sprouted from every surface. Earthquakes shook it, and an entire section of wall collapsed. Tons of travertine blocks were hauled away and used to build palaces and churches.

The Roman Empire fell to the barbarians at the end of the fifth century, but the Colosseum remained standing. Despite centuries of tumultuous change, it still stands today. It's the best-known building in all of Rome, and one of the most famous in the world. Archaeologists continue to study its remarkable engineering and solid construction. Its design is imitated every time a sports stadium is built.

It's easy to admire the people who, nearly 2,000 years ago, were able to construct such an extraordinary building, but it's very hard to understand the appalling purpose for which they built it.

If you enter the Colosseum today, and walk through the echoing high-ceilinged corridors, and climb the steep stairs, you feel something of what the Romans must have experienced long ago. Anticipation mounts as you pass from the dim arched passages and out into the dazzling sunlight of the seats. Even in its ruined state, the first glimpse of the arena below is undeniably exciting. It's possible to imagine what it must have been like echoing with the sounds of the crowd, the musicians, and the wild animals. The Colosseum was built to thrill, and it still does.

But that does not change the fact that what went on for so many centuries in that famous arena was grotesque and inhuman, despicable by any standards. It's horrifying to imagine Romans cheering while people and animals were tortured to death. It's disturbing and confusing to think that the same people who created countless brilliant works of art and architecture also delighted in public murder. For us today, the Colosseum is both an example of the greatness of ancient Rome and a symbol of its terrible brutality.

England

France

Spain

Rome

Greece

Middle East

Mediterranean Sea

North Africa

Egypt

*The area in purple is the territory controlled by
the Roman Empire at the height of its power.*

523 Venationes banned

476 Roman Empire falls

404 Gladiatorial combat banned

500

400

300

200

100

81-96 Domitian ruled
79-81 Titus ruled
69-79 Vespasian ruled
54-68 A.D. Nero ruled

A.D.
0
B.C.

27 B.C.–14 A.D Augustus ruled

80 Colosseum officially opened

64 A.D. Great fire in Rome

27 B.C. Roman Empire founded

44 Julius Caesar killed

100

200

264 First gladiatorial combat in Rome

300

400

500

509 Roman Republic founded

600

700

725 Rome founded

bestiarius— animal fighter

damnati ad bestiam— condemned to be executed by wild animals

essedarius— gladiator who fought from a chariot

hoplomachus— large and strong gladiator who fought with the heaviest shield and armor

lanista— agent who trained and supplied gladiators for combat

ludi (plural of ludus)— gladiatorial games sponsored by the emperor on official holidays

ludus— a school for gladiators

munera— gladiatorial games held at funerals in honor of a dead person

patrician— noble aristocrat

plebeian— commoner

Porta Libitina—Gate of the Dead

retiarius— gladiator who fought with a trident and a net, but without a helmet

rudis— wooden sword symbolizing a gladiator's release from the arena

secutor— gladiator who fought with a sword, a rectangular shield, and a helmet, often against a retiarius

spoliarium— room where gladiators' bodies were stripped of armor

Thracian—Grecian style gladiator who fought with a short curved sword and a round shield

tribune— representative elected by plebeians

velarium— awning which shaded the seats in an amphitheater

venationes— wild animal fights

FACTS

Length of Colosseum–620 feet

Width of Colosseum–415

Height of Colosseum–160 feet

Area covered by Colosseum–6 acres

Length of arena–280 feet

Width of arena–175 feet

INDEX

CREDITS

Art Resource, NY: *p. 40*

Giraudon/Art Resource,.NY: *p. 32*

Erich Lessing/Art Resource, NY: *p. 31*

Fernando Bueno/The Image Bank: *p. 44*

Michael Racz: *pp. 4-5, 7, 10, 13, 14, 17, 18, 21, 22, 25, 26-29, 35, 36, 43*

Scala/Art Resource: NY: *pp. 9, 39*

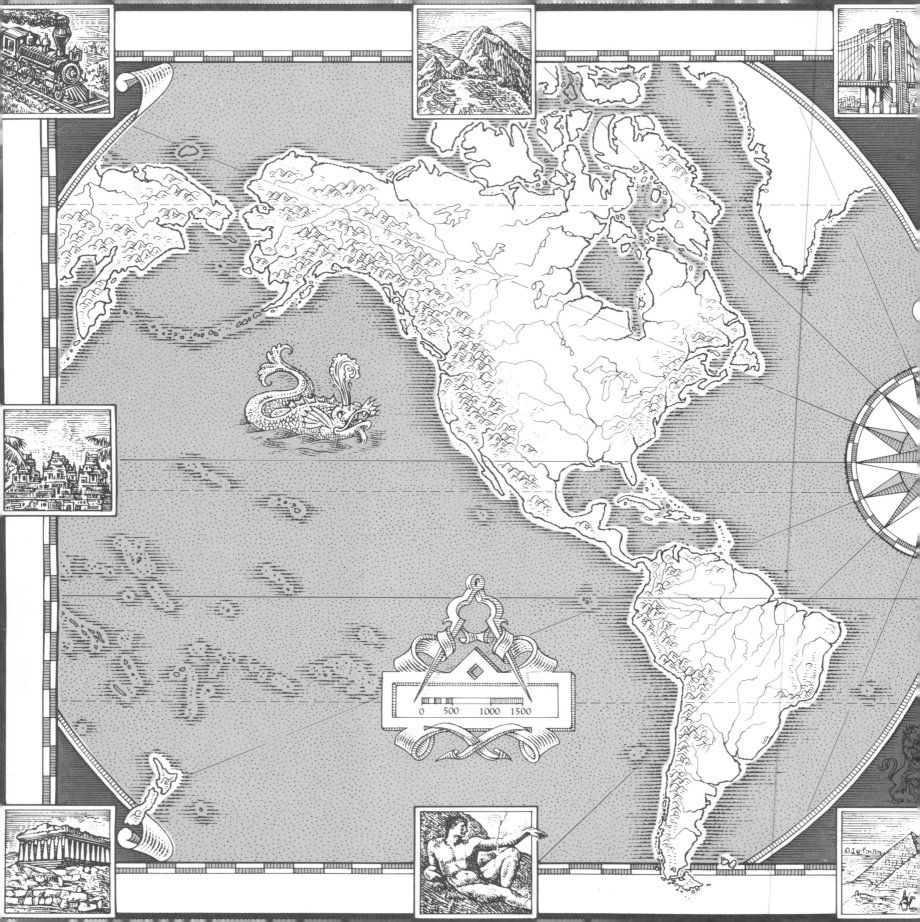

0 500 1000 1500